Musings of
Mina

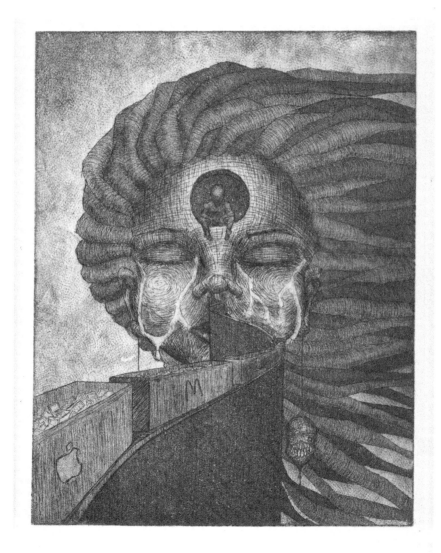

BY LISA LI

Musings of a Modern Mind

Lisa Li

Copyright © 2022 Lisa Li

ISBN: 9798415908479

For my Relatives and Friends worldwide for their support during such a difficult time here on Earth.

CONTENTS

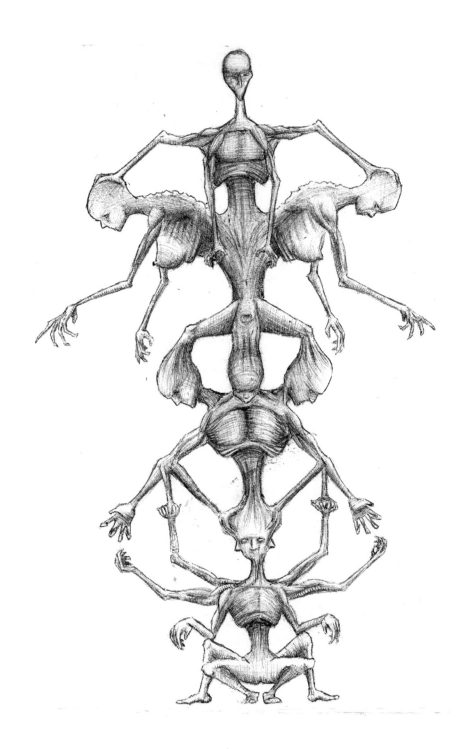

ACKNOWLEDGMENTS

Marco Poma for letting me use his fantastic old Art and always being such a good friend and inspiration along the road.

Lee Phoenix for being the best bestie reading and editing when your so busy studying psychology you still make time for me.

Dad for the proof reading, love you most.

It's an honour

And an opportunity
To be oneself
To free oneself

...LIFE

As I wait,

Procrastinate,

The pain starts to alleviate,

Through written word,

A channelled verb,

Alchemizing all,

Do not disturb

Here is the book my wisdom stirred.

To tell the tale of a modern world,

That bent and broke and bled and turned,

Till we all woke up and broke the curse,

Of a modern hell that couldn't be worse

As the art healed us — the pain reversed.

Modern slaves, Expansive universe.

✦

Are we looking at our life through a filter ?

Through a filter of fear

Fear of death

Fear of a new world order

Fear of sickness

Fear of loneliness

Fear fear fear

Or a stagnant filter of monotony

Same old same old

Nothing fresh or exciting

Work sleep repeat.

Boredom.

We are living in precious times

Where more than ever people are waking up to seek more
from life

We don't have to live by society's rules

I repeat

We don't have to live by society's rules

Stop watching the programme

Literally

If something is making you fearful

Stop watching it

There is a life full of love

That can be lived with just as much rigour

As those love and fun stained memories of youth

Remember them ?

Before you put on those fear stained glasses...

Who put those onto you ?
Worries passed from adults
Pressures passed from society
Fear spread by media
We live in precious times where more and more are looking
to heal
And dissolve those filters of fear
Drain those stagnant inner ponds
From the clogged emotions and traumas of past
And clear the lens to see...
There is nothing to fear here.
We are creators of our own realities
We get to choose you see
Take back the controls
Feel your feet on the ground
Go walk in nature
The system is abusing you
Some can cope with this abuse
Others can less and less
How I wish to open trauma rehabilitation centres
To heal us from this mess.

✦

We learn through suffering
By feeling our own edges, we can redefine ourselves again and again
Learning resilience and humility
Through self practise or some sort of training
Or through bowing to life's sometimes harsh teachings
Can we uncover the treasure
The wisdom found through the galvanising of life's hot fires
Melting the hard metal cages that have formed around our hearts
Dissolving rigid concepts, opinions and structures.
Without such a furnace we cannot alchemise.
With a life too comfortable and unchanging.
Too easy, straight forward and predictable.
We get complacent and gluttonous.
Trapped in the comfortable confines of societies template,
The determined monotony
Year after year, provoking the need for drama and bullshit just to feel something, anything.
Only through the shaking and waking that life's unpredictable earthquakes can bring us
Through grief, through devastation,
Can we be shaken from our sleepy stagnant wasteful and weary ways
Cracking our hearts wide open once more.

And these years the whole earth is shaking.
No more can we be sleeping lions.
In this paradise of endless quantum creativity,
No more can stagnant structures hold

Until it all crumbles down...
Everything
Every concept
Every barrier
Every attachment...
We are fighting a losing battle !!

A forced awakening
Who would have thought ?!
After all the bullshit
We have been taught
The world would turn upon its head
A spiritual journey
We're on instead.
Who's to say who's right? who's wrong ?
Ridiculous concepts
They were all along
Beyond everything
Beyond all the lies
Beyond all the struggle
Beyond all the cries
A hardcore awakening breaking us through

Dark nights of the soul
Rebirthing anew

✦

Can it be trauma and pain are teachers, to guide us
back and back to walking on this earth more gently....
Each time shocking us awake,
Reminding us again, and again,
To turn back...
Towards peace and softness ..
To find harmony
Within safer more nourishing spaces with stronger
boundaries
Equal giving and receiving
To each be a peaceful energy on this earth…
Gaia is steady on her feet
Can we tune in
And add to this stability
Lovingly tending to all our wounds
And thanking them for their sweet reminders
Reminders for softness
Reminders for balance
Reminders for peace
Letting go of what we are used to
To move towards that which we want

✦

What more do we need but the birds and the bees.... and the sycamore trees, being safe being free, To live in peace and harmony......

✦

The way where we push and shove is not the way
The way where we try to figure it all out
Or become so attached to the outcome
Is not the way
The way where we work all day
And value things over freedom
Where we monopolise
Where we pick at and people please
Is not the way....

The way is the middle way

This is the way where the daffodils bloom
And the birds make love
Where the weather rolls in and out
A baby is born
And where tears spontaneously fall
Where adventures happen
And lightning strikes
Where plans are unraveled by a laughing god
Where death cracks you open
Where art is created
Music and dance free-styled
And poems are written

We lost our way... by trying to control
With science pulling things apart and
Needing to know

When the egos lead
And the greedy pushed and shoved
And made money their mission

But in losing our way
We forgot to play
We destroyed the land
And we micromanaged our day
We even chased all the love away
We forgot all the stories
We lost all the wisdom

But the way cannot be lost
With each newborn child
Consciousness is reborn
Reminding the adults
Of magic and presence
Until we let our small minds teach them
Telling them what's best
Showing them our way

The way we got lost
The way that it is
But the forgotten way
Is in spontaneous bliss

Don't lead the way
With your head or your greed
Or we won't have clean rivers

Or smiling mouths to feed
We will destroy our planet
If we continue this habit

The middle way is here
Once you become clear
Theres nothing to fear
You will smile ear to
Ear

✦

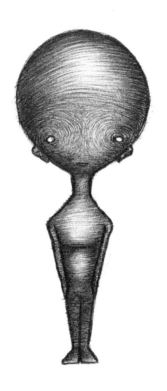

Love with your eyes wide open.

✦

Us that are light workers
are here to spread light
we are not here to fight
or here to be right
or have long discussions
dragging on through the night
we are here to transform
like the dusk turns to dawn
with our conscious precision
our emotional disposition
with our training in alchemy
who knew it'd turn out to be
the necessary transformation
global alchemy across all nations
see that's why we're spread out
in all corners, have no doubt
in all collectives, all families
all professions, hidden alchemy
so don't fear, don't dismay
'cos with each passing day
light is growing
and its showing
theres no slowing
may as well sing
spread the love
spread the vibes
let your hearts come alive

channel the good energy
let it spread from you and me
rippling out
have no doubt
good vibes entraining others
all our sisters and our brothers
all our fathers and our mothers
the new earth — it is upon us.

It's going to be a bit messy
as we all find our truths
as we express the unexpressed
we reclaim our choices
sometimes pushing away strongly
or turning away from it all
or running off into solitude
so we can feel ourselves once more
needing complete silence
or darkness
or lack
to feel true wants
detached from the conditioned preferences
or opinions we have been programmed with
or agreements we have absorbed
to become sovereign
to become clear
it is a messy game
its not always a clean switch
into the middle way
sometimes its an unblocking of a damn stood for a
thousand lifetimes
a cry of a thousand stifled cries
the energy collective of all those too scared to cry out
as the energy unblocks
and we unblock
to become clear vessels

Expect a messy unravelling…

✦

When walking in ones truth in these unstable times,
I'm realising more clearly how this affects the status quo,
And why it causes such a stir,
Such a resistance and conflict...
People are not used to truth,
And if truth comes it's often softened with such niceties, people pleasing to a fault.
Softened blows when sometimes blows are just what's needed to create alchemy.
Kids were seen as trouble makers
Who would go against "the system"
Really they were the truth seekers...
The bringers of light,
The change makers,
And what do we do? Silence them or make them bad.
Conflicting ideas create change.
They bring creativity.
Chaos to shake up and wake up...
To disintegrate old ideas and rigid structures,
To bring in the new,
To create better foundations,
Dismantling the old,
Building a more conscious world...
So when conflicting ideas are presented to you...
Or a different perspective that challenges your rigid world view...

Of how things are...
How things have always been,
...Instead of shaming the ones bringing an alternate truth,
Instead of outcasting them or ridiculing them,
Or calling them a trouble maker,
Try to remember...
These are the new ideas that could create a better Earth.
These are the truths that are uncovering the shadows,
Uncovering the things we could not see,
The fears, the unconscious…
Sometimes we need to be made uncomfortable…
These are the brave souls not afraid to challenge the old
ways,
So don't Shame and blame them,
This only invokes the trouble maker and defence
mechanisms,
From those already walking an uncomfortable new path,
Triggering their wounds of being the "black sheep"
They are not slaves to the system.
Try to listen and allow their view,
Because we all need change in this world,
Surely we can agree on that.
And without those speaking the conflicting truths,
We will continue on the rigid road we have been already
walking along way too long.

◆

This beautiful life...

✦

The invisible magical conquests and hurdles achieved in this lifetime are insurmountable.... Maybe one day I can express it in a book, give it the explanation it deserves, as opposed to standing with empty hands to show, but the soul knows......

And what the soul remembers is all we can ever take forwards,

Not money, not cars with expensive ego satisfying number plates, Not land we have pegged as "ours"....We will laugh and cringe at such notions in the after life, We will see them as so wasteful and clueless. No, what the soul can learn and grow through stands the test of time, the test of lifetimes... through the trials and tribulations, breaking through the maya, seeing beyond the illusion. Such a difficult path, but so worth it... And beyond the hard work, such days like these in magical paradise.

✦

Letting go of the past

Over and over
Letting old structures crumble
Rigid ideas and conditioning
Conditions..... arranged around fears
Should's and shouldn'ts
My way or the highway
Individuality hidden behind Personality
The tired old ways that weren't working anyway
The I am rights, that dimmed others lights
The listening through filters of fear and hidden monsters
of the night
Separation
Screens cleansed to see the hidden unification
All an illusion
Polarity confusion
Letting go of the past
Letting lives we wanted crumble allowing the lives that
were meant to be lived appear...
Letting go of it all
Dying unto oneself
Over and over
Letting go to reveal
Only presence and love
This is how we heal.

What happened to honesty ?

Integrity ?
being who you appear to be ?
its plain to see
how it looks more importantly
than how it is
how it is
how is it?
That what looks so solid
is built on a house of cards
and I can see the weak links
so blatantly
but others turn away rather than see
your missing out don't u see?
Life is not this
don't you see
don't you see
honestly
everyone is free
but what truly pains me
is the falseness you see
people just happily
rather turn the other cheek
they refuse to speak
on truth that is right there
hidden behind the locked doors
bored nights
and house chores
get the wine out
looking fine out
Instagram
what a sham.   ✦

Anxiety blocks creativity....

✦

May I stand in my truth

With loving kindness...
May I stand firmly in my own truth
No matter the reaction
No matter the retaliation
May I support myself with the same loving kindness and
support that I try to offer to others
May I have my own back
May I respect their truth
And be aware of the filters it may be spoken through
May I not take things personal
May I have firm boundaries
And self awareness not to retaliate
To say when somebody is overstepping the mark
When someone is assuming, blaming and accusing,
To kindly and clearly observe it
Without being drawn into another's drama
Drama and chaos in this world right now is rife
Mirroring energies
And whilst those still cling to egoic structures
To avoidance
To addictions and escapism
Running from the very feelings that are here to break and
shake us
To evolve us
The emotions that will take us
collectively forwards into new ways of being

when we integrate them and accept them
Letting them dissolve our walls and wake us
Rather than blaming them onto someone else
Everything happens for a reason when you are in the flow
In the unraveling of consciousness
Every feeling
Every trigger
Every circumstance is here for our collective evolution
Can we accept? Can we allow? Can we appreciate the
process??
Every urge is channelling creativity supporting the
evolution
When we move freely not clinging to the sides and the
structures controlling how it needs to be
Attached.
Instead Surrendering
Letting it fall
We free fall with life
With self and free expression
We allow ourselves to feel and take the time to notice what
unravels
So much is unravelling just now
It's very easy to get tangled up in bullshit
And quick reactions
Rather than staying sovereign
And knowing that these inner energies are everything and
all that we have
And from what we will create

And realising others can never be to blame
For the experiences and lessons we have attracted into our
own lives
Strong boundaries are needed
Much self love
Standing strong in one's own corner
Not being drawn into the fight
Sending love to those triggered into pain and blame
Standing in love and acceptance
And truth
Giving space for expansion
As we witness the collective shadow work,
Consciously being faced
And unconsciously being avoided,
As the earth alchemises.

The shadow is where your treasures and hidden energies lie,
When daring to look with a really keen eye
The lost and hurt parts we discover
Keep turning inwards
Trust the process
Whilst here on earth we will recover.

✦

Will we even recognise who we once were before these years began?... What a gut wrenching spell binding time here on earth !! Thank you for the support of our ancestors to get us this far........

✦

So many layers to healing from abuse

Not only is it healing from the damn abuse itself

And forgiving those who did it

Seeing how they got it

And then it's realising where we can be abusing others

Through this taught behaviour

This mismanagement of pain

Breaking the circuit.

Healing that.

Then

When you think you're bloody healed…

It's healing the awareness

And having boundaries.

Around letting partners repeat that same behaviour to you….

Abuse sneaking in through the back door

Knowing you're worth more

Everyone is worth more

Than receiving abuse

Than perpetuating that cycle

Passing on the hurt

To the next generations

To partners

To others

Fuck.

✦

There's very good reason why people are fighting against losing their rights.

Look at Afghanistan.

We are already a world of war veterans....
Whilst trauma carries 7 generations at cellular level, not many of us are spared histories of being under attack,
For some the trauma lies more fresh in their bones, just a couple generations, some are still at war.
When will we realise, greed over this earth's resources and politics is destroying us all.
While the rich cling tightly to their possessions comfortably watching others suffer. And run off to the moon gloating, while the rest watch them in disgust and shudder at the absolute ignorance of it all.
Pouring money into trauma healing, into wellness and healing spaces, so those of us can work to heal us deeply like we so badly need.
Hurt people hurt people.
Feed a man a fish, he will be fed a day…
Heal his trauma, his world and everyone around him will change.
This healing ripples out.
You want the world to change ?
You want the world to be kinder?
Put your money where your mouth is.

It starts with you.
Heal yourself.
And if you've healed yourself, what can you do to help heal others?
This is not the time for looking away,
Escapism through shopping…
We are here to make a change
All of us together.

The man stood alone counting his riches
at these times is a gluttonous fool and shame on him.

✦

Everything Is under construction...

Just because someone's offended, doesn't mean they are right.

Being honest is often kinder than trying to just be nice.

Life moves in mysterious ways,

And lessons are never straight forward.

Remember to not give anything more energy than it deserves.

To give people and experiences space to breathe and alchemise.

To align myself with those who feel good to my soul, people, businesses, places, things...

To get my energy correct first before making a move.

Just because someone acts like a self righteous martyr, they can most certainly be causing a drama through assuming and projection of their disowned shadow.

They can also be not as sincere as they seem.

Perception is literally everything.

We are most definitely here to embody the new energy on this planet and create a new earth.

✦

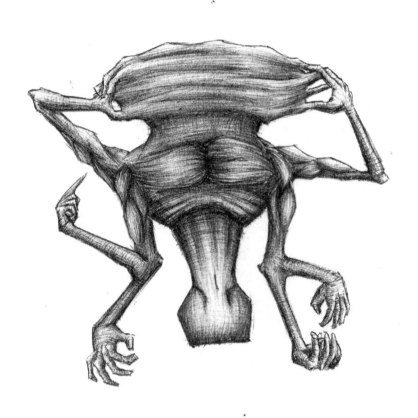

If we are serious about healing the world
We have to get serious about healing ourself
The self beyond the busyness
Beyond the coping mechanisms
Beyond the addictions
The reasons we stay small or hidden,
Safe or reliant.
Distracted or dormant
To get serious we have to start to be honest.
Honest with where we are
How we are feeling
And begin "the work"
Meditation uncovers true feelings
Yoga and breathwork inner pain.
Relationships uncover much much more
What is your lifetimes work ?

Clearing space,

Letting go of the old,

Wiping the slate clean..... and expecting better

✦

So by this stage.....

Maybe here in England we have already paid a lot of our karmic debt…

With the long suffering hours in dead end jobs, through the struggle, and restricted rigid ways of living,

Through the sickness or the pain and aches,

By the disconnection and the loneliness,

Or the long cold grey winters,

The hard working class,

Or by the old money getting cold and stagnant,

Realising it's loneliness and how energy needs to move......

By the pain of losing loved ones who escaped thru addictions, sickness or suicide.

Maybe we already passed thru the heavy karmic load that this country inherited throughout the generations,

Maybe we suffered enough that we finally let go.

If you escaped society already then nothing much can really affect you.

If you let go of your attachments.

And there's too many of us.

More waking steadily,

More awareness.

At first they cling and kick and fight and blame and fear,

Till they realise it's all futile.

And to see the change you gotta be the change,

You cannot change anyone else,

Only yourself,

And find your own niche part of the tapestry, that actually
can add to this world, be it creatively or by just being you in
whatever it is you do,
Do it well and make sure it's what you love.
It's a simple shift that echoes loudly through your ancestral
line as they all rejoice that you finally broke free…
That you heard your calling.
And stepped into place.
I only consider this, as I watch other parts of the world in
full fight and collapse,
And yet here feels still, and reborn in many ways,
A slow wave awakening rolling in consistent.
Maybe we suffered enough.
Maybe we dropped the armouring.
Or at least we are in the process.

Sunny days and blue skies…
Make me realise,
There's more than to react to silly lies,
More inner work that can be done,
In your small bubble so much fun,
Don't listen to news,
And all the blues
When life's what you make it
And it's just begun.

✦

The view from the afternoon.....

✦

To be transparent ///

To tell it like it is.....
Not like it's not, and hide behind lies and false smiles and
shifty eyes
To mean what you say
And you say what you mean
Not distorted truth
Behind a smoke screen
We can use our discernment
To judge what is true
When there's smoke and mirrors
Who has a clue?
To be transparent
Is just what we need
Media scripts
Companies and their greed
When things aren't transparent
Who can tell what ?
Of course we won't listen
We haven't forgot...
Until things are honest
And integrity restored
We are within our rights
To separate from the horde //
It's vital to demand a different way
Where they say what they mean

And they mean what they say...
When people are selfish
They're stale and they suffer
To share there is magic
When we care for each other

For those who are awake
In this amazing time
Disconnect from the system
And reconnect to the divine...♥

✦

It's not weak to take a pause to look deeper at what is hurting you.

It's not pathetic to take that time and recognise that sensitivity.

It's wise — knowing that "staying strong" and holding it together is a waste of energy.

It's truly strong to get vulnerable with ones self
To really listen to look what hurts and ask deeply — why?

Because until these hidden wounds and anxieties are addressed, there will always be a chink in your armour…

A chink that drags u back to keep enquiring.
To keep self soothing.
To a deeper understanding, of who you are and why… ?

A deeper knowing of oneself and what one needs to feel good.

Not lost in an imaginary future or nostalgic past…
But facing the now, feeling it all and embracing all that is, in the face of love.

Heaven on earth starts from within.
Use this time wisely.

✦

Work smarter and harder.

✦

Awakening is ugly and hard and painful.....

and many of us have already had the worst thing possible happen to us… We've already lost it all, or been broken to what looked beyond repair........ We don't fear loss or death. This awakening started for some of us a long time ago......... The harsh reality of life already faced...... To face death, to face disappointment, loneliness, cruelty, devastation........... The path of trauma can be a path to enlightenment. Is there truly any other way ??

.... For the many who have been used to comfort and protection, used to excess and even gluttony.... This may be the first time to face fear of death. Fear of loss of loved ones. Fear of loneliness and seclusion. Fear of boredom, or hopelessness...... Fear of pain.

Remember how that felt? The first time…

Ripples of repetitive shock and fear programming daily on the news.
Don't tell me that news channels don't know the damage this causes.
The relentless depressive statements,… The continuous hopelessness.
Don't tell me they are not aware what that does to the mental health of a society.
Continuous stress, without time to process the last thing.
We know being negative breeds negativity and hopelessness
This is nothing new !!

TURN OFF YOUR TV.

If you have food in your cupboards, and heating or a roof over your head.... family around you, someone to call, a livelihood,
breath in your lungs and life in your body then

COUNT YOUR BLESSINGS.
Don't wait till it's all taken away to realise what you had.
Enjoy each and every day,
Life is fragile and precious and can be taken at any moment.
And that's true with or without a pandemic.
Nature is still open,
The birds are still singing
And inner transformation is happening…

I cannot help but feel excited by the shift in consciousness this earth clearly needed.
There are many many many of us clearing ancestral trauma, integrating shadow and facing ourselves continuously, to raise our vibration.... and become the powerful creators we have always been, but with consciousness !!!

Do not be disheartened if it's hard,.... growth is damn hard, but eventually always worth it ..... Can we be thankful for this growth?
Can we be thankful for all what we have?
Can we be loving to how we are feeling, without further stress of listening to more negativity on top of it?
A time for strong boundaries perhaps,
A time to be conscious of what we are consuming....
Where is our focus ?

Just Breathe...

✦

We are living in veryyy interesting times //

Can we be channels to bring in divine justice?
Channels to balance divine order ...?
What is justice in an evolved world ??
To encourage growth and new understanding through
support?
Educating and encouraging change ?
Or to continue to punish and shame ?.. //
Can we shift the energy ???
Through alchemy //
Love and understanding //
We cannot judge, can we ??
We cannot judge the process…
or know what's another's path.

CAN WE TRUST THE PROCESS AND
CONTINUALLY COME BACK TO THE LIGHT ?

✦

Anytime we focus or point our attention towards someone or something, that is a sacred honour and gift of our energy.
Life is short, there are infinite things we could be focusing our attention on.
What are we choosing to send energy to?
What are we choosing to interact with?
Who and what deserves our precious energy?

✦

Can you find Acceptance ?

Can you find Approval ?

Can you find Appreciation.........?

........For whatever it is that you are going through,
personally and collectively.....
This is the fastest way to find harmony with what is........
and some would say, everything is happening for a reason,
To support yours and our evolution.

✦

I am light I am love I am one.

✦

STRIFE…

Beyond the illusion

Beyond the bullshit
Beyond the negative beliefs
The lack of self worth
Beyond the same old reactions to the same old triggers
The excuses
The stories
The fears
The toxicity
The traumas
The projections
The distractions
And the addictions....

Beyond all of that illusion
Is everything you were born to be
To have
And to experience
With clear vision
Seen from eyes of pure love

So Detox from it all
Cleanse anything that is not love from your system
Let go of every attachment
And every thought form
Every disappointment
And excuse
Let the old energy die

So the new can be reborn
And in that fresh presence we find the present
The freedom and the energy
The life we were born for
The moment where we can begin to create in joy.........

✦

All that glitters is not gold.

✦

Living with CPTSD is literally insane

Anything can set you off
A harsh word
Hunger
A slightly snappy tone
Confusion
Discomfort
Heat
Fear
Crowds
Loud sounds
The list goes on...
Triggering an inner response well out proportion to the situation
Inner painful reactions
A feeling and need to scream, cry, run
An inner conflict
Invisible to the eye
Undetectable except to the one with the internal bomb gone off
Hard to breathe
Impossible to ignore
An urge to project and blame the outer thing for the inner pain.
... In this world we learn to be tough, to suppress, to cope, to remain calm
To ignore.
But with CPTSD this can go against the healing flow... and the need to resolve.
But trying to fit in we can learn to shove this reaction down
Swallowed and suppressed

This can further entangle pain deep into the body,
Like an inner volcano threatening to blow I often would sit and act normal
Finding ways to release the pressure without causing more harm has been my aim and method to live in life more peacefully
Because an outburst can cause a forest fire
Full destruction
Often met with no understanding
Or understandably defensiveness,
blame, anger, shame
Things can escalate to unimaginable levels
No... better to "act normal"
And release in some socially accepted or unnoticed way
Breathing it out with a slight tone
Shaking
Moving the body with noise
Or heading off to sit in a toilet cubicle to silently scream
Better than to SNAP
Underwater screaming is a great and hidden method
Or singing at the top of the lungs (more easy disguised)
My own history of "causing drama" or feeling misunderstood prefers this incognito method of release.
As tensions rise in this earths reality and in a climate of overall stunted emotion,
so do the use of pharmaceuticals to numb these triggers and sadly suicides also do rise.
Everyone suffers from PTSD in my opinion, to some level, only to varying degrees..
This is why I live and breathe (literally) breathwork.
I hold space to help people truly release all of this inner tension and suppression.

If we listen to our bodies there is so much needing to
speak.
Diving deep to see what has been unseen,
Through breath sound and movement — our energy is
returned to us, along with our relaxation.
We feel to heal...
The stuck energy we move to e-motion...

✦

PURGE +RELEASE

Negativity
Outdated beliefs
Judgements
Defence mechanisms
Control dramas
Opinions
Hatred
Hurt
Shame
Blame
Fears
Toxicity
Tension and stress
Anger
Grief
All that's hiding underneath ....
*** A collective dark night of the soul is upon us.
Clear out what's not serving you &
Integrate your shadow
How much pressure do you need?
How bad does it need to get?
Before turning inwards
>>><<<

✦

GROUNDED

as inner unstable structures crumble
stripped back to the foundations
all that was known on shaky ground
torn back to new beginnings

REBIRTH
Laying stronger roots
nourishing the soil with kindness and love
strengthening
maturing

CAN WE BE THE LIGHT
in the darkness
in the midst of the chaos
in the eye of the storm
can we find peace and happiness
can we ripple out joy

THIS NEW WORLD is a vibration that starts from
within !!!

✦

Wow what an exciting time of biggg shifts and quantum leaps into a world of our own magical creations....... It's like time is collapsing and the past dissolving, revealing a clearer and clearer present, whittling out the projections and limitations, alchemising soooo many dense layers of energy... Generations and centuries of it, let alone lifetimes.....So so much to be processed...... even just in this life time. //

✦

We can't see the depths of what we are healing....
((not for the faint hearted — trigger warning****))

The invisible breaths, reaching the invisible energies,
Breathing down deep into childhoods and past lives...........
Into shattered nervous systems
And fragmented memories...
Clearing the way for deeper depths to be reached and felt.
Conscious breaths,
Diving deeper,
Bringing pain up to the surface to be loved and held,
Shining light on what was forgotten, hidden and
submerged.
Reclaiming lost energies.
Bringing back a stronger frequency,
A brighter light and a more wholesome loving accepting
self,
Integrated.
Walking forwards in a different energy.

I'm realising more and more how this world is energetically
armoured, with fake smiles and "I'm all rights" whilst
quietly people go walking off to sea to commit suicide.
Communities are starting to become aware of the need for
more communication and support,...... showing more
compassion for the silent struggles of others, having
experienced the same first hand, yet still lacking the tools
and efforts required for the extent of healing the trauma

carried by most people. Carried and coped with via elaborate defence mechanisms and solitude..... addictions and avoidance....

Until dis-ease manifests.

Then it's a whole different ball game.

No one truly escaping how they feel or choose to heal in the end.

What I'm also realising, is the more you stand steady in truth,

Having taken down the armouring and healed...

Having swam down into your inner depths, retrieved the broken parts, sung danced and loved them back together, facing shadows, fears and memories.....

So you can stand more steady in your truth,

Then you will trigger the fears and shadows of others.

Your very energy will drive out their darkness.

Shining a light into their own hidden chambers, without even trying...

Confronting what they are hiding from.

And then there's the words...

This is not all just love and light, and certainly not for the faint hearted.

Shadow work is intense,

It's confronting, complex.... and often challenging well armoured wounds protected by egoic opinions of how things should be.

Good and bad. Right and wrong. Black and white.

A complex obstacle course of unraveling consciousness,
always looking to blame the pain on something or someone
outside of them having caused it.
Rather than to feel what has been touched, and allow for
expansion.
My energy can destroy villages and start forest fires.
And I know I'm carrying the remembrance of having done
just that, and then being made an example of for doing so.
Burnt, killed, tortured.
I know and I feel it, ...and I heal it.
The more confronting the truth, the deeper the trigger, the
harder the blame, and the defence tactics...... the
retaliation..... often with martyrdom.
I've been outed for speaking only my truth so so many
times.
Expressing how I felt, when others would lie.
Having a different perspective.
Owning my processes publicly, as I have nothing to hide.
Outed I have been, as I trigger something uncomfortable
deep inside them they are not ready to face.
Or conscious enough to be aware of.
In the past I have retaliated, feeling the triggers of past
lives, burnt at the stake, whole towns turned against me,
This was the feeling stirred up inside me,
And thus creating the explosive reactions it triggered in
myself.
I see it.
For just speaking truth.

Or standing up for some different perspective.
So much pain and inner turmoil has exploded, when the fingers point from the one disliking my truth.
When truly it was always said with loving open honesty.
Yet as a result I would give them what they wanted,
The evidence they needed to say that I am this and I am that.
Burning their house down.
I am realising this now ever more clear, to walk with more awareness as to not take on the blame.
Not to retaliate, but to heal my own finger pointing wounds in private.
Not to listen to their words, and to see beyond their tactics.
As to why they are pushing their pain away.
As to why they are reacting and projecting.
To hear beyond their words.
To accept it with peace.

We do not know the depths of what we or another is healing.

The depth of trauma is invisible pain.
And it is also a very personal game.
It's easy to point fingers, and outsource your blame .....
especially to ones so willing to step in the flame.
But until we dig deep and own our own shame,
This cycle of hurt will remain the same.

✦

Be the lighthouse — not the storm

✦

Traveling slower, breathing deeper, loving harder…

✦

RIGHTEOUS ANGER ...

When you can see beyond the bullshit at the pure manipulation.
When you fear for the health of loved ones — when you are seeing and hearing of reactions and deaths from the you know what.
From nurses working in hospitals full of said reactions.
From real people.
Groups of people.
Friends of friends real videos shaking uncontrollably on their couch.

RIGHTEOUS ANGER......

When said loved ones laugh in your face like you're crazy.
When u see the new neurological disorders of people you know,
and hear of deaths where people say it was "after the you know what "
When it's so obvious the amount of gaslighting on TV.
When people are abusive, and feel it's ok to be abusive, because they are "doing the right thing".
And you — to question, apparently are not.

When friends have had to leave their homes to escape new laws.

And others have been stranded away from family.

When people have lost jobs or been manipulated into things they didn't want to do to keep jobs.

When groups on facebook are created for people trying to detox from the thing they didn't want, because it messed up their immune system.

RIGHTEOUS RAGE...

When people have power who really should not,
Who openly don't care about nature,
Who don't really care about people as individuals,
Stories of police doing absolutely bullshit things for no reason other than to scare people to do as their told,
said police smirking, enjoying their power.
What the hell kind of protection is this ?? This is no longer protection this is misuse of power

When all the while we are not being taken care of by no caring leaders.
Quite the opposite.
Whilst they have their opulent parties, using repulsive Eton messes to be the face in the front of their pantomime.
Whilst they cause more chaos.
Whilst huge companies get richer.
Whilst they up their surveillance.

RIGHTEOUS RAGE.....

We have been slaves to a system that has not served us for
long enough.
And we are realising the unfairness.
And so this is a last ditch attempt at control and
manipulation.
Yet we cannot even say a thing.
Our rights removed.
Our voices gaslit and silenced or muted.
Laws to protest changed.
Blamed on the very ones who are caring the most.
Or caring at all...............

RIGHTEOUS RAGE....

We have been convinced anger is a negative emotion.
It is not.
It is a sign that our boundaries have been violated.
It's a sign we have been mistreated.
Without it we are just docile minions who can be persuaded
to do anything.
Intuition is when we can listen to our emotional guidance
system.
To know when we are being violated.
To know we are being coerced, deceived or mistreated.
We have been dumbed down — don't you see?
Entertained, drugged and distracted.
TV sugar sex.

If we are not in touch with our emotions we are not in touch with our intuition.
We are already a long time zombified, by relentless Netflix dramas and subdued by a need for alcohol, cigarettes, and sugar.

Tell me Im crazy to be angry ?
Tell me I should just do as I'm told ?

Go 1 week without overeating, watching TV, drinking alcohol, distracting yourself, overworking/keeping busy.

Face your emotions for 1 week head on, without taking off the edge — no weed, no painkillers, no sugar.
Reconnect to the true nature of yourself and of the earth, not the TV or government guidelines.
Then maybe I'll listen to you.
Until that point, I do not believe you are seeing things clearly.

✦

Argue for your limitations, and they shall be yours.

✦

What it's like to hide in a castle of pride

egoic walls built high
looking down and around
no care to be found
prides size pumped up with tall lies
faking strength
to any length
uncaring
spiteful staring
voice blaring
know it all
secretly feeling small
chest pumped out to make themselves tall
what a fool
prides lies and cunning eyes fools them all.

✦

What happens to a society when those who are
allowed to inspire and held up as heroes,
Are only those who support a narrative,
An agenda,
A big business corporation where we are all turned into
customers,
Advertised at,
Entertained,
Hypnotised and kept in fear by reruns of news stories,
Focusing on the worst of humanity,
Lulled into a false sense of security,
Taught to believe we have NOTHING TO ENVY.
Thank god we live here,
Thank god we are given these drugs for cheap,
And these minimal resources,
It could be so much worse…
All the time unknowingly blind sided,
Kept sick to fill people's pockets,
Poison in foods and water.
Taxed heavily.
Greed driven rulers overpaid and most certainly under
delivering.
Zero wisdom or ethics.
Lying, coercing, manipulating.

Are we awake yet?

I used to see the state of things and feel so fucked up and
sad honestly,
At the true possibilities of how we could be living,
And then the harsh reality,
A hostile world everyone playing their part,
Kept poor and disempowered,
Angry and blaming.
Hating each other.
Full of trauma and manipulated by these wounds.
Projecting it at neighbours or loved ones,
Or at those that the news tell u to hate.
Addicted.

Are we awake yet ?

People going on and on about the you know what,
When honestly…… Everybody is anyways sick.
From many many diseases,
Ignoring anxieties,
Numbing out.
Sad stories and tales of misery….
Heartbroken and depressed.
Slave driven and stressed.
When we don't have to live this way.
Not any more.
Times are changing, thank God.
The people have the power,
We have never seen this so obvious,

Huge protests echo across the world,
Whilst the media remains silent.
Still focusing on some crap to keep you angry.
Blaming.
Disempowered.
In many ways here in UK we have a saving grace.
We probably can't be silenced or bullied.
We are aggressive and we have that white supremest British
empire leg up thats had us at least believing we were free...
But our media is hardcore.
Like a fucking Hollywood — tightly scripted,
Keeping us sweet.
How could these well loved celebrities or religiously
watched news programmes be biased?!

You realise if you stop watching it your world is fine right ?
You have only yourself to deal with.
To heal.
TVs smashed up in the streets might be the kind of protest
I'd like to see.
Newspapers burning on bonfires.
Because can we surely not see by now....?
They are keeping you angry.
Keeping you fearful.
Keeping you blaming each other.
Beyond that, what is there?
Beyond all the bullshit......
....All the blame and hurt and pain...

There is freedom.

And it's only a choice away.

A choice to heal and to take your power back.

We should never ever be trusting these heroes, or these leaders who try to convince us we have nothing to envy.

Life is improving, in many ways.

We are evolving and realising better ways to live.

This is why the world is closing in on us (so says the media)

These are last attempts to keep the control.

What lengths will they go to ?

To keep people quiet,

Make them disappear....?

Do not be so naive.

Stop watching the news.

You are being played.

Over and over.

Step out of the game, and let the cards fall where they may…

Whichever way you burn through the fires of
life
Be it presence
Be it discipline
Be it suffering
Through illness or committed study
Or hard work
Or hard art
Or the breaking of your heart
Or through shattered life
Or broken dreams
Make it all worth while
Don't waste a drop of precious pain
To fuel the fire
Of life
Use it to burn away
What stands between
You and the unseen..........

Having lots of money ain't nothin.

Not if you don't do good with it.
Anything good. Something...
to help others less fortune.
Sat on hoards of money is still lack.
This is still living in the energy of not enough that is
hurting people and destroying the world.
Meaning wealth is hoarded.
Not shared.
I tell you what is somethin....
Digging yourself out of a dark hole,
Climbing out from generations of suppressed energy and
trauma,
No matter how it looks.
Trauma comes in many shades...
Stagnant fearful ways.
Healing your beliefs,
And expanding your awareness,
Becoming more connected and seeing the good and the
magic in
Everyone and everything.
Feeling blessed and fortunate
and connecting to nature.
Doing good things and caring for people —
That is something.
Not getting paid a healthy check to keep tight lipped or do
dodgy deals,

Or manipulate whole countries into remaining stuck in an old system.
One that keeps people poor and less than.
Whilst you get paid lots,
Or hang onto lots,
Sat laughing and dumb,
Oblivious,
Arguing and worrying over crap, when clearly there are things that can be done,
And there are people with much better morals,
Ethics,
and wisdom
Who should be in charge...
Who should have power...
Who could use that wealth
In healthier ways.
Healthy for the environment,
Healthy for each other...
Equal
Aware
Kind
Giving…
Not grabbing.
No sitting on a bunch of money ain't shit,
No matter how you got it.
Nor a bunch of land if you're not going to do something good with it.
Resources are meant to be shared.

Money is meant to be a tool for change.

Energetic exchange.

Addiction to earning or spending does not equal abundance.

Until the world sees its fearful and hoarding ways there will always be poverty.

Don't blame the big guys at the top or some distant elite.

Look how your relationship is with money,

With resources,

With energy.

Soon people gonna choke on all that stagnant energy.

Energy needs to move

Life teaches everyone in the end.

Whilst the indigenous continue praying and respecting the lands and the animals.

Sitting patiently till we admit how wrong we have been all along..........

✦

Tunnels of my mind...

✦

Sadness running like dark black rivers
Meandering through my soul
Thick tar like tunnels and channels
Coursing thru memories
Tainting everything with its thick sad sludge.
Dragging me down
Poisoning the present
Until one day
I realize...
That the sadness was all love.
Grief of "shoulda been different"
Was a knowing that I deserved better...
We all deserved better.
Grief from lost ones I loved,
Really was echoing the weight of that love.
The tears from what had happened,
Was really showing a deep love and care for myself...
Urging me to strive for more peace
More respect
More fairness
More truth.
And without that amount of love
That passionate care
Turned pain of what should not have been...
I would not have propelled myself forwards,
To new territory,
New situations,

To do things differently...
The shedding of past to look for better ways.
Only love can demand better,
Only love searches for more,
For different
No that sadness was not sadness at all...
It was deep pools of love
Reminding me that there is more
There is different
stronger
Deeper
Lovelier.
Kinder.
To swim further for....
And when I realised those deep sorrows was really love...
The waters began to clear,
The poison drained
The grief lifted
The channels opened.
Nothing to be sad for....
This was just the way of learning.
Through experiences
And journeys taken.
Hard paths
Painful endings
Lost love.
Gaining wisdom
Evolving me and

Guiding me forwards...
Through those watery channels
Alchemising the water
Into pure rivers of gold.

✦

Some of the oldest of souls have been buried in the
toughest of stories,
Right in the trenches of family dysfunction.
or up to the eyeballs in generational drama…
poverty and trauma,
This was not for no reason!!
That the oldest of souls chose these scenarios,
to bury themselves deep in stagnant rigid dense energy,
needing huge amounts of effort to break themselves out,
forgetting of course why they are here,
and who they are,
but driven by an insatiable need to be free!!…
Alchemising the densest of energy into light,
which is exactly what they are here for,
to transform this dark world into one that is more holy.
To shine light in the dusty shadows,
breathing space into suffocated shallows,
to reflect back truth to those who have long forgotten,
to bring awareness where fakeness rules,
and absolute tools,
manage to rule countries,
bumbling and dense,
somehow from old money,
or absolute luck of bunking with the right people in
boarding school, did they make their way to being prime
puppet,
with puppeteers hands well up their ass,

misguided and crass,
with a nice healthy pay check,
glutenous and gullible…
Whilst the oldest of souls are still digging relentlessly,
unconfidently somehow blinded to their worth and their
huge potential, remembering little by little as they clean off
the dirt, relentlessly digging themselves outwards and
upwards towards the light.........

✦

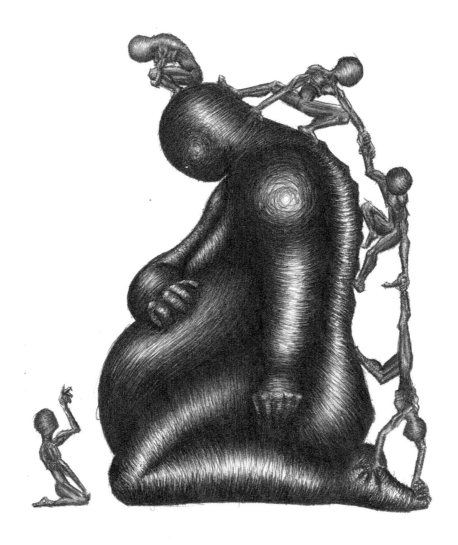

I walk through life like a blade

Knife cutting through bullshit

Speaking my truth, how I see it with love.
Standing up for myself and my views, when needed
Honouring my emotions when I feel that clear nudge or
harsh shove.
Holding people accountable for perceived injustices
When I feel mistreated
Disrespected
Abused or pushed out.
Sometimes.....
Using righteous anger,
The form of anger Jesus used.
I am not afraid to express…
My Kali.
My rage.
Even though it's been massively shamed.
When I'm expressing my hurt.
Not to cause trouble
Not to hurt people
But to live in truth.
And to sharpen this edge was not easy.
I spent a long time in silence
In meditation
Working thru my layers

My pain body and triggers
My armouring
From past traumas
Working thru my projections
So I could know myself and my truth
And it's still a practice.
I am human.
But I have sharpened this blade long enough now.
To trust in my truth and my definition.
To be able to listen to my emotions as a guidance system.
And I'm learning more to know when to move away into
silence.
But being, walking and talking this way
Is not for the faint hearted.
It provokes all kinds of reactions
Manipulations
Assumptions turned judgments
Mistreatment
Lashing out
Even violence
Defence mechanisms
And projections.
Which all used to trigger me.
What I'm learning is to stand solid.
Have strong enough boundaries to deflect such attacks
With a balanced response.
Not giving any more energy than necessary.
But staying with the truth.

It's a practice.
Much like meditation.
Tracking truth.
Being present.
And responding precisely and accordingly
Respecting and honouring myself and others
Where we can do better
Calling each other out when needed.
So we can learn
So we can evolve
In this world full with projected pain and torment
In this world of fake personas and self proclaimed
shamans and martyrs
Where we can't bare smell our own shit
So we project it.
Where the enemy is kept way outside of us.
Where we are fragmented into only the acceptable parts
that we show
Shadows held at a distance
Not whole.

People pleasing and putting up with such mistreatment

Easily manipulated pain bodies by media sources

Easily controlled and docile
The walking dead.
No we don't like the truth
It can be shocking to us to feel this keen blade

And sure, there are easier ways to live.
Like putting our feet up watching Netflix and being passive
aggressive behind each other's backs.
Behind false smiles and numb anxious bodies.
But how we do one thing is how we do everything.
And soon it becomes a constant flow.
And so — if I choose to live in my truth and present to
life's challenges,
Then that's in every situation,
Every conversation.
Sometimes it's just not worth it.
Sure.
The reaction can be exponentially out of proportion.
But worth it ?
Isn't shifting energy into light always worth it?
In such darkened times.
To move us forwards out of this stagnant old way of being.
To learn to get along nicer.
To learn to stop being a self righteous twat and actually
walk our talk.
To become more aware of how we effect others.
This is a practice.
And I am also human.
Sometimes people's reactions and distortions provoke me.
Sometimes I lose track of the truth.
Sometimes I let things slide and later suffer.
Or give things way too much energy than they deserve,
But it's a practice.

And my blade is getting keener.

And my insecurities around this are getting less.

As I'm learning to trust my emotions and this blade.

As I'm learning to flow in truth.

In a world that will tell u to hush now,

Keep your head down and say nothing.

Go along with it for an easy life.

Whatever they do or tell ya.

However they mistreat ya.

But I don't think I came here for an easy life.

I think I came here to create change.

And I shall never be silenced.

But I will learn more precisely when to move into it rather than to give ammunition.

✦

Tracking the truth....

Sometimes can be a challenge…

When assumptions get made, and over reactions,

people looking through unclear lenses,

hearing things with biased ears,

or seeing with full projection.

Its important to track the truth,

without giving more energy to things than they deserve.

The truth within yourself.

Honouring where you are at.

Whilst having the courage to stand up for whats right.

Without getting tangled into another's projection.

Its a challenge.

Being too nice can literally get you nowhere,

and further down the line, can result in a lack of respect,

as you are quite clearly a push over.

Tracking the truth,

and speaking your truth,

in the moment,

standing up for yourself and for what is right,

not just doing things for ease....

letting things slide...

Its a fine balance and tightrope to walk.

We cannot hide from our truth no more.

It can have huge consequence,

It can ripple forward and effect futures, personal and collective.

Truth's being shaken to the surface and thrust in our faces.
We can no longer stick our heads in the sand,
and pretend everything is fine.
Now is the time to face our truth and speak it,
whilst honouring other perspectives,
whilst staying in balance............................ It's a challenge.

✦

We really need to change the whole system, schooling system and parenting.... delving way deeper into developmental trauma and just mind blown. How can we judge or be angry at anyone when this kind of programming is so deeply embedded into us all?! Deep shadowy powerful years for self healing if you are on that vibe. This world needs healing deeply and I feel we're gona see many extreme behaviours as we are being pushed beyond our limits..... Awareness and softness is key as we head into lockdown number 2 here in UK, God help us lol but I'm excited to see what alchemy can happen as we turn in once more...

Emotions buried alive don't die…

✦

Which B O U N D A R I E S are necessary?

An imaginary line
Keeping away unwanted guests
Those in need
Those that might take our stuff
Closed minds and closed borders
Germs travel through air
They don't care for passports
Invisible to border control //
Inner B O U N D A R I E S
What we choose to take inside us
What thoughts
What programmes
Internalising the deflected emotions of others
Listening to their uncontrolled dialogue
The news
The fear
Choosing what we listen to
What energies we're around
What beliefs we don't have to listen to
Protection from the inside
Autonomy //
B O U N D A R I E S can protect and strengthen when
used wisely
Incoming disturbance can weaken
Antagonistic energies
Repetitive negativity

Unwelcome views and influence
Energetic and unseen
Keep your mind body and soul clean //

✦

Walls //

When too many boundaries are crossed
Walls become necessary for protection
Invisible boundaries trampled over
Creating just as invisible yet necessary walls
We must honour those walls and their reason for being
created
And respect until they feel ready to come down
Slowly gaining the trust that they are now unnecessary
Allowing them the time it needs to slowly dismantle
Gradually dissolving
Into open safe arms when trust is regained
Not trampled over because now we know better
Walls came up for a reason
And trust takes time
Respect the process
With honour and patience

✦

From Love to hate in a heartbeat, when one refuses to feel the pain of triggers.......
Learn to process the pain and you can heal a multitude of life's wounds... growing and thriving in this ever expanding wholeness...

...

This is how we heal the world from the inside out, not sticking to the old programmes of blame and hate....
We are coming from the dark ages into the light of consciousness, and the process isn't easy — but it's what we're here for. To shine light onto the darkness and alchemise. Not to stay lost in a world of defence mechanisms and ego....
Be brave enough to feel, ask for support if you are struggling but let's not pretend any more this is what we are going through...
If we have a lot to heal it's because our souls journey can handle it.

✦

A strong ego messes up your perception
Ego is just armouring
Protection from the harsh reality that you are living
Or that you once lived.
Armour erected.
Defence mechanisms learnt and continued use…
Projecting some past unhealed trauma
Onto the life you live and the people surrounding you.
A warped perception of reality because of an ego you
won't dismantle
A false reality
Deceiving yourself
Stuck in ego and denial
Dragging old traumas along life's beautiful path
Destroying it on your way
All the beautiful gifts and passage ways you don't even see
Too full and blown up with past stories and life's scars //
Life is a battle
But we choose what armour we continue to carry
The war is over now
So why do we cling to this armour ? //
When your roots have been damaged
Or if they are missing
Or your branches have been held back or destroyed during
old storms
Still you can go back to the source
To the beginning

To even before
To Nourish the seed
Tend to the soil
Water the roots
Even the forgotten ones that are most rotten
Sing and speak lovingly to your tree
Admire its flowers
Tend it back to life
Give it the strength and nourishment it never had
The Attention and love
For It's never too late //

— The hardest wars make the toughest soldiers…

Can you stop aligning with the chaos of the world ??
With the drama and the karma
With rumours and fears of "Big Pharma" //
And instead align with your true self.
Dropping deeper into the peace that lies,
In the knowing of a higher consciousness,
A consciousness that is turning you again and again to go
inwards.
A consciousness that is showing you presence,
Beyond presence into a steady balance.
Do not align with the madness and the chaos of the
world //
The circus on the surface....
Feel the instability of it...
The shakiness and escalated emotional reaction,
Realign again and again
To that deeper knowing
That ever flowing
Light of love and pure awareness...
And from that place,
Dream a new world into reality
Project that peace onto your world
Every inch of it.
Onto your future
Reminding others of a higher and more steady vibration
Give them something more blessed to attune to.

Hold your beautiful vision strong
Be grateful for the changes ahead
For it is done //
This is how we awaken
We be the change and mobilise it into reality….

✦

Respond don't react
When people attack //

Most people don't like to live in truth
They live in white lies and faked smiles
Or egotistic guile
Someone living in their truth exposes their shadow
Triggered parts they haven't accepted within themselves
Parts they cannot handle
Or see theirselves as separate from
So they may project it upon you
Judging you
Blaming you
Fearing you
Putting words in your mouth
Or giving meanings to your words
Or calling you a trouble maker
Because it doesn't fit their status quo
The socially acceptable way to go
Chained up in conformity
They can't handle free

Respond don't react
Truth is what's needed in this disassociated world
It brings up the shadow for integration
We cannot side step this any more
Boxing ourselves in to perfect and nice

People pleasing and ego easing
It may look chaotic
It may not be obvious or nicely packaged
But light work is not just simply light
It is also shadow
We cannot fake our way to enlightenment
Or love n light our way to wholeness
Or nice our way to healing...
Unless we own our own triggers
And see the bigger picture
How the ego try to trick ya
Everything is perfect
In the unraveling of consciousness
Without triggers
Without shadow
We cannot heal
It's all apart of the big reveal…

So respond don't react
When people attack
And say things like "your supposed to be a healer"
Don't give them your energy
So they have their proof
Your reaction
Another distraction
Don't take on this label
Because it is nothing to do with you
It's their shadow unowned

Their unconsciousness
They don't have a clue
Try to breathe
And see what's underneath
No one said this would be a journey of ease
Your not here to people please //

✦

Shame and guilt like roots twisted deep into my soul

Fossilised in my energy I pull it out like weeds with new awareness
Like how is this programming ?
And what am I without it ?
A rusty cage holding me in shape, the wrong shape
One not flowing with my being or any kind of love
More bent into fear, oppression, rejection and shock
As I continue to bring light to it — new expansion arises
With the cracking of bones I learn to rest deeper
Relax into the soul of my being
Under the pressure cooker that is LIFE.

✦

Shadow consciousness

Smashing up against each other
Like waves crashing on a cliff
Projection and confusion
Too much disillusion
People pleasing
Avoiding healing
Through avoidance of truth
Imbalanced visions casting their view
What we judge without — we judge within
Different people — different skin
When embracing all we can truly begin
Not pointing blame
But turning in //
>>>>><<<<<

✦

CRITICAL TIMES

CRITICAL DAYS
PSYCHOLOGICAL WARFARE CALLS FOR
SPIRITUAL ACTIVISM...
Can we have compassion for those who have hurt us ?
CAN WE FORGIVE ??
Those that must be so hurt they have to over compensate
with money things power control...
Can we find in our hearts compassion for that ???
Without wishing to do to them as they do to us ??
Compassion is the highest form of love...
Is the oppressor just as hurt as the oppressed deep down??
This world needs LOVE AND HEALING...
Unless we want to continue to be manipulated by our
wounds
manipulated against each other
We gotta FEEL IT TO HEAL IT
And PURGE !!
We ALL have ancestral trauma
and we never thought we would live through a time on
EARTH like this !!!
WE ARE CO-CREATING
This is the most important time so far here on EARTH
REMEMBER YOUR POWER
INTENTION IS EVERYTHING
FEEL TO HEAL
MOVE THE ENERGIES

CLEAR OUT OLD ENERGIES
UPGRADE YOUR THINKING…
REMEMBER YOUR MAGIC
CALL IN THE WORLD YOU WANT TO SEE…
IMAGINE THE BEST POSSIBLE OUTCOME

DEMAND PEACE ON EARTH //

Does our outer conflict reflect our inner conflict ?

Do we over protect ?
Building walls to keep us safe and seperate...
Do we lead with defence
at any sign of perceived danger?
How can we build bridges instead of walls ?
Where we meet in the middle
and conflict can be discussed
like healthy adults...
Where both sides are listened to
— honoured for their personal pain
and respected for their needs...
Witnessed without judgment so the pain can transform
coming to a space where both can have their needs met
Not fighting over the same toy like children
But sharing
Seeing the fear behind the aggression
Seeing the trauma behind the defensiveness...
When there is media poking you again and again right in
your trigger
Stirring up over and over unresolved generational trauma
that BOTH SIDES HAVE !!!
This can be said in any case
Israel and Palestine
vaxers and anti vaxers
fears played upon
fears of death
fears of losing freedom
fears of losing family
fears fears fears
Triggered traumas from old wounds passed down through
the generations...

Wounds we don't even know we are carrying!
Where is the media that is trying to repair the conflict ?
Where is the government trying to unite difference of
opinion ?
Where is the reparation ??

THINK FOR YOURSELF
QUESTION AUTHORITY

✦

Let it all fall down...

✦

So many layers to address………
Nothing is ever just black and white…..
The complexities of trauma
Unprocessed since many generations
Being triggered to the surface
On what do we now focus?
The brainwashing
The manipulation
The separation
The dehumanisation
The blame
The hate
The racism
If the world is on fire then the Middle East is in hell
Corrupt politicians
Terrorists as well
Both sides feuding
Who starts it who can tell
Everyone looking for someone to blame
While the true culprits stay hidden and
as Bob Dylan said "We're just a pawn in their game !!!"

✦

With our ancestors behind us..
The elements all around us..
And pacha mama supporting us…

How can we feel powerless ?!!

✦

THRIVE

Can you open up to life ?
Can you let what is coming to you find you ?
Can you allow the lessons ?
the twists and turns,
the triggers that unravel your ego…
Without blaming them on the other,
Without reaching for whats next
Without doing
but allowing…
Allowing life to flow,
and the way to show
without forcing and pushing
controlling whats so…
Can you read subtle queues
and the hints and clues
Can you allow what you love
to be your muse…
When we open up and allow
what is to be
everything is perfect
If you let go, you will see…

✦

The old world is gone.
And the new world is here.
Can u feel it?
It's more raw,
More real,
And it's coming from us.
We are the centre of our own universe,
The experiences we attract,
The acquaintances.
The abundance.
The addictions don't work any more.
The distractions lose their joy.
Nowhere to run,
Just an impending truth,
That can and will shatter realities.
Those basing worth on what's outside
Nobody's watching any more.
No more hiding from what's within.
Can be in heaven and feels like hell.
Or hell can feel like heaven.
The new earth is for sure here.
The old is for sure dead and buried.
More will wake up.
Many will hang on,
Egos attached, desperate.
May as well let go and flow.
With the end of codependence.

The end of duality.
The new earth is here.
Buckle up

As I roam this earth, shedding layers, leaving pieces of my heart in the hands of those I came to love, gaining beautiful memories and losing judgements…

Going deeper into my soul and further along this dusty road, I walk.

Contemplating…

No one ever has walked this exact same path as mine.

And probably no one else ever will.

What unique exquisite lives we lead…..

Growing up in the west is like growing up in the land of instant gratification... wanting the success without the effort, wanting the wealth without the work, wanting the finished product without the creation... people taking partners and making babies without first becoming an adult, or learning how to be first an individual....

For me I will take my sweet ass time to recover from that programme and let the nature teach me and grow me... Learning the patience of Mother Earth, healing and strengthening my roots, laying a strong foundation, searching out lost wisdom and connecting to the elements and seasons... There's no rush in this life to throw up and build anything fast in a hurry for it all to come crashing down !! Be patient with yourself... take all the time u need... even if it's a lifetime !!

✦

The ever expanding moment...

✦

We need the lows to reach for the highs...
We need weakness to ask for strength...
We need sickness to truly want health...
We need loneliness to seek companionship...
We need the pain to look for the love...
Life is about the CONTRAST
We need boredom to imagine new adventures...
To stretch the imagination...
To evolve and grow, each time seeking more,
reaching further, expanding and creating....
Accepting the fluidity of it all....
Enjoying the ride....

✦

How long must we watch the same movie.....?

Looking through the same lens
Smeared from past pain and fears
Projecting onto reality
Creating more of the same
Can we take responsibility for cleaning our own lens?
Looking with eyes of innocence and peace
Not blame and hate
As the world kicks up more of the same
Will we retaliate?
Will we step into the same energy?
You did this
They did that
Or will we walk in a new energy?
Of peace...
Not so easy when it's on your doorstep I know
Not so easy when people point fingers
Not so easy when everyone around you is also traumatised I know
But this is a problem of trauma begetting trauma begetting trauma...
We must turn inwards and heal
Then walk forwards differently
We cannot fight for peace
We can only peace for peace

Is this not an inside job?
We can also pray for peace
And we can speak for peace
And dance for peace
And love for peace
And make art for peace
And be the peace
To try to understand the others perspective
To lay down our weapons
To be done with tit for tat
So difficult as a collective
So difficult as a whole country or ethnicity
But maybe you were only ever supposed to be in
charge of your own energy…
And that energy be a shining lighthouse
In a world full of storm //

Animals are really such angels on this earth....... so innocent and pure, present and loving........ whether it's the sweet little birds singing their songs all day long, or the wild animals just going about their cute lives........ and pets are angels sent from heaven.... into our lives just at the right time, to teach us how to love, how to be calm, how to build trust, and how to open our hearts......... to receive their love is such a blessing, their acceptance and adoration, and it never gets easier when one of your baby angels goes back to heaven. I definitely believe animals are here for reasons we don't always understand, and the grieving can heal us so deeply when we just allow that depth of sorrow to just tear through us until it's done..... sometimes takes weeks, months even, but in its wake, leaving so much more room for love. Because only the power of loving something that much can truly break our hearts open...... They are such a gift in this life, and I feel so lucky to have known each and every one of those pure hearted angels

✦

In between worlds — New Portals //

✦

Today I had a realisation,

A deeper realisation should I say
Of the effect the TV news truly had on me
Growing up with it in the corner of the room
On pretty much constant
Intermittent news throughout each day
I had a deeper realisation, that how as a child
This damaged me greatly
Trauma I'm still unraveling from
Absorbing the tragedies of the earth
In my most vulnerable state
Being in the comfort of home
Open and relaxed
Seeing violence
Women murdered
Kids abducted
Polluted seas and poisoned animals
It came to me today just how deeply that affected
me
Without the emotional support to process
Accepted as normal
To see this type of thing
How much all of that got into my brain
Convincing me of such a sad hopeless world we
live in
Creating fears I would not have crossed paths with
otherwise

Fears much bigger than me…
Creating some kind of sick twisted comfort and
safety sat there on my settee
Yet at the same time poisoning my mind with fear
and sadness
I have only just really understood this pain I have
been carrying
on such a deep level
and the effect that TV box had on me
Had on us…
Do we know we have been so brainwashed ?
Do you know if you're still watching it how
brainwashed you're still being ?
War hate fear blame…
I wonder how the world would look differently if
we didn't have this relentless drama pumped into
our eyes and ears
Certain opinions repeated
Certain versions of certain events
Would we be more present ?
Would we be more empathetic and less
armoured ?
Less defensive and fearful ?
Less opinionated and judgemental
If you took away everything you saw on the news,
and only had your own eyes and ears to teach you
Taking away the radio too....

The gossiping tabloids
Well I'm sure we wouldn't all be as terrified of this
illness that's for sure.

If we took away the TV
What kind of world would it be ?
Would we be more free ?
When it's just you and me...

✦

What is FREEDOM ?? To be free, isn't to eat anything and everything and consume and devour and indulge, glutinous in too much excess and have it all. Freedom is not to use all there is on offer to excess and to wander aimlessly from experience to experience, trust me I tried it. freedom is not the inability to choose or to be constantly inundated with options. Freedom is not to be trapped, yet it is not to run. running away is no more of a prison than that of 4 walls…

I believe in freedom from attachment. To things, to people, to places, to outcomes, yet it doesn't mean never to choose. To be free and choosing are not separate from the other. To choose is to put roots. To invest. To focus, to nourish. Freedom and choosing, they are not 2 seperate things— Excess is not freedom, nor is addiction. You can be free in the mind locked in a prison cell. Freedom is not escapism. To be addicted, to experience all is not a free life. It can be even more trapping to have endless options and stimulation and addiction to more. Nourishing only apathy, when you can have more, the things have less meaning. Could having less be actually having more? With more focused energy things grow more beautiful, appreciation emerges. For what we have, not for what else ?

To be free to be free from how else it can be
To be content and happy is freedom for me……

✦

Growing up as a female in a patriarchal world that does not respect the feminine is quite literally torture and so damaging in a multitude of ways...... The feminine nature is reflected in the nature of our planet..... It is not male, it is not ordered, or consistent, straight forward or unlimited for pillaging..... It has seasons, it flows, it responds to nurture and appreciation, allowed to grow wild and free..... It nurtures us in response and provides everything man needs, is a home to all and gives unimaginable beauty. She does not need fixing. She cannot be controlled, conformed, micromanaged, abused. Otherwise she becomes barren, stark, ugly, malnourished and can even turn on us in anger and chaos. Look at the malnourished soil from overuse, look at palm tree plantations, polluted waters, forest fires and floods...... She is not a place to ditch your rubbish, or to be hidden away under concrete or suffocated under fake grass (astonishes me anyone would choose fake grass)....... She is to be respected, she is fragile yet strong, kind loving and healing, unpredictable and chaotic. Takes time and patience to understand. Like the women on this planet..... Brought up in a masculine world that does not respect the feminine. Told we're too much, we're draining, a head ache..... Confusing, and need fixing..... Unsupported and malnourished, overworked and stressed.... Causing sickness in their nervous systems and wombs... She is sensitive and her body has a delicate balance we are all trying to master !! Women are gentle yet strong, we have cycles like nature and are unpredictably exciting...... We, like nature, should be respected and nurtured...... We are not men, we are not the same as men, and for balance on this planet we should not be trying to be.

Men can learn a lot from the oracle that is women, our sensitivity and allergy to bullshit. Our awareness of feeling, when things are not quite right. Until Women and Mother Nature are respected,... this planet run by male ego will not be in balance. We need to heal the feminine, and we need to be respected.

Then watch the planet transform.

✦

What if love never feels safe?

What if it was never ever meant to give you that? What if no matter how many profound insights you have, how many amazingly powerful awakening experiences you collect, or how convinced you become that you have it all together… that you will always be at risk for a beloved to come in and show you how vulnerable you really are? And to reveal to you once and for all that your vulnerability is not a weakness, or a part of you that needs to be transcended, but rather is the gift you have to offer this world.

What if love comes raging into your life, in all its forms and expressions, not to offer security and ground, but to reveal your wholeness? Love would never ask you to surrender your vulnerability, to spin tales of an awakening where you will remain immune from heartbreak, or to dream fantasies of resolution, security, safety, and ground.

Love wants you to get naked. To get gooey. To get sticky. To get messy. To be willing to be torn apart. To die and be reborn again, over and over and over. When you are unclothed, of all of your spiritual concepts… love will show you what you really are. When the known crumbles away, all that remains is your burning heart. There is nothing more alive than that. There is nothing more sacred than that.

You are longing for freedom. You are burning up inside. You are becoming a fool for love. As soon as the sadness has gone, the despair has subsided, the fear has passed, you say: Then I will be free, then I will know love, then I will open my heart all the way. Then I will be awakened.

But friend, this freedom is here. It is in the centre of your grief, if you will only touch it. It is in the pouring out of your sadness, showering this world with your heart-essence. It is locked up inside your fear, hidden in your rage, and overflowing in your loneliness. Love is everywhere and is coming for you. Will you see it even in the most unexpected places?

As long as you have a body you are at risk of heartbreak. As you awaken, prepare to feel more, not less. Love will never ask you to transcend this human form; only to come closer. Remove your clothing. See the beauty and the magnificence that has taken shape as you.

✦

Sometimes you gotta close a door to open a window…

✦

As consciousness expanding…
As planets aligning, pressure building, pushing us deep into the wedge of energetic dark corners…
Seeing shadow we never saw,
As the ego fights to survive…
Battling to be right, furious at others perspective. Fearful of what, death? Losing others? Losing freedom? Being told off? Being lied to?
Shhhh.
This is a spiritual journey…
These patterns do not serve, these hidden violences,
There is a life beyond all the bullshit.
Unpicking and shining light of consciousness deeply into these predicaments.
These reactions, these aversions, these urges…
What energy is stuck there within this fury?
Can we see it all ??
Do we dare to truly look ?
Huge shadow like chunks of armour from the dark ages breaking off me lately…
Such a deep process I am totally amazed at the beauty of it all.
Literally the old world is falling away…
We were all made for bigger things
Life does not have to be a struggle
As we shift with the frequency of the planet
stay with an open heart

Breathe
And allow this process.
Be silent
Be still
Rest.

✦

Do we hold people in their past to be the same as they were before?
Do we project into the future — expectation of past disappointments
fears and mistrust
defence mechanisms
defending us from what once was
ineffectively creating what will be
carrying past into future
big heavy rocks we drag along,
keeping us the good
— the victim
proof and our projection
but don't we change?
and if we change, doesn't everything and everyone else also?
and anyway aren't we all one ?
So that what we so adamantly judge,
surely is a part of us
a part we so reject and disown
blame, shame, criticise, spite
this is an opportunity for rebirth
amidst a spiritual war
an evolution of consciousness
bringing light to all that is hidden in shadow
integrating all

All that we are, that we once were, and all that we swore we would never be…

✦

Imagine if this country got reWilded

— If people got sick of working long hours to buy expensive clothing when they already have wardrobes full, and instead turned to the land to protect it, to allow it to regrow.... Instead of giving up 40 hours a week to pay for expensive 2 week holidays to nourish their soul, they nourished through their daily lives, and growing the food they eat.... If they got sick of sitting in cars and traffic and chose to live more local, walking, biking, if they slowed their lives down.... less pollution, less greed, less speed.... // Instead of hoarding everything for themselves, they shared and honoured the earth that belongs to no one and is home to us all, ... If they got sick of the TV and news and radio blues.... and they remembered to nourish through connecting with nature, music, and art, ...and instead of looking good they learned how to feel good, ... Imagine if this country was re-wilded ..... how beautiful and magical it could be...

✦

Forgiveness releases any expectation that things could have been any different....

✦

Can we take responsibility for all we have created ??
in our individual lives and on a collective level…
Where have we put ourselves in the hands of others??
Others who may not have had our best interests at heart.
Where have we been hurt by this?
How can we heal our pain, and step up into truly caring for ourselves?
Speaking our needs
Individually and collectively
How can we best communicate that ???
Is blame shame outrage hate and fear the way to communicate?
Do we need to turn away and meet our own needs first?
Find our own balance
Become SOVEREIGN
Be responsible for our own emotions and state of mind.
Stabilise…
Not look outside for answers,
Because the world is imbalanced.
How can we support our own unique balance, and then project that out into the world?
Speak our needs
Our opinions in a balanced way
Not tainted with resentment, blame and aggression.
Until we find balance inside, we will keep playing that imbalance out into the world.

Meditation, yoga, tai chi, nature, painting, a million things can support our balance…
We are the change we wanna see in the world
Its nobodies fault we are evolving…
— So lets EVOLVE !

We have been Creators creating asleep
Thus creating chaos
Through lenses of unprocessed trauma
Age old beliefs
Skewed thought patterns
Without awareness
Creating chaos
What does it mean to awaken?
To become aware
To see the ugly truth
To see our patterns
Our limiting beliefs
Rewrite the story
In current limbo
Dreaming big dreams amidst the external 3D chaos
Reprogramming
Changing our beliefs
Being accountable for our creations
Choosing to do better
We are life's artists

✦

Kindness is the cure

✦

New life smashes old paradigms //
Brave souls carried to places and situations that force growth,
ever expanding and growing in strength, lessons learned through perceived mistakes... growing more self aware, exposure of weakness — chance of becoming more strong, yet humble to go more gently with new awareness. Lessons don't get repeated.
History can be erased in the mind and heart of a true conscious warrior.
Don't judge me on who I was yesterday, because today I'm above. //

"No man ever steps in the same river twice, for it's not the same river and he's not the same man." - Heraclitus

✦

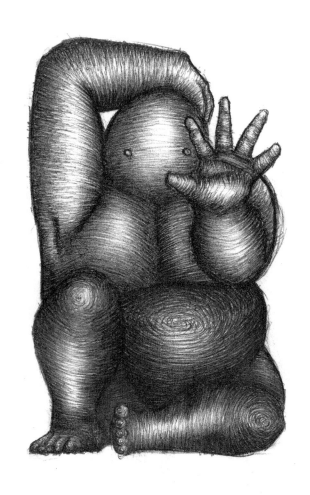

You can be 21 and be carrying each one of those
heavy years
weighing on your back
your chest
your heart
all the dysfunctional memories
all those fears
layers upon layers
old stories
adding you decades of years
heavy wrinkles in your frown
dark around the eyes
a heaviness in energy or weight
so walk on light in your years
shedding those memories
not looking through old fears
walking more present
lighter
more free of the past
and you can be reborn again and again
and again //

✦

GAIA/GOD is all around us, draw from her strength, appreciate her beauty, communicate with her POWERFUL energies, and ask for her knowledge and guidance.

APPRECIATE her elements that wash away your fears, blow away the cobwebs and ground yourself in her stability, feel her consistent support under your feet in every moment.

ACKNOWLEDGE how her fires can burn away that which doesn't serve you and breathe in her nourishing airs…

CONNECT to her essence and she will guide you and move you in the direction of your path…

You are not alone, she is all around you, in you and a part of you.

HEAVEN is not just on earth, ---- IT IS EARTH !!!

✦

Nature Imitated Art.

✦

Wounded FraGmENtS of the soul

....display their wounds through feelings //
Irritations show me where I need more soothing
fears show me where I need more comfort/reassurance
anger shows me where I need more love and understanding
loneliness where I need more support
mistrust where I need more faith.
These feelings are sign posts
like a road map showing you the way...
To love yourself from the inside out
follow your way back home...
and love yourself back together !!

Full circle //

Thoughts spiral back closer to truth...
year after year,
day after day...
allowing the bullshit to slip away...

✦

Everything is coming in perfect timing

all what we need
even the stillness and aloneness
sometimes the most terrifying gift
to observe the struggle, than trying to escape
grasping at thoughts, needs
worry and anxiety
fears and doubts
forced further into stillness
deeper
to escape the madness
until…
finally surrender
into peace and understanding

✦

When I don't smoke or drink or distract myself

There is a pressure

From the inside

This pressure is the alchemising of old energies

The combustion of creativity

The portal for inspiration

The more I sit

The more I wait

The more I breathe and watch and feel

All the answers are inside of me

The map

The momentum

The mission

It is not about physical steps but more the energetic tone you can get into before the steps take place…

✦

Forgotten roots left in dusty undernourished soils.... Beneath our feet as we grew up..... clueless to the power and strength accessible, so within our reach yet in our blind spot. Looking straight ahead never under or behind. Grasping. Reaching forward. Building empires on desert lands. Accumulating false riches leaving true nourishment left to wither. Forgotten roots left in malnourished soils beneath. Soft cries of forgotten souls and histories untold, a shallow future and forgotten past. Lineage no more. Out for oneself. //
Stood alone. With the latest iPhone.

✦

Letting nature take its course.... //

✦

The New Traveller Culture.

The ones Brave enough to turn their backs on a broken fractured society's sick ways to explore and learn from all corners of the earth.

The ones that threw themselves into the abyss, then carved out for themselves a new life, resurrecting and recreating themselves from within.

Step by step loving their broken pieces back together, manifesting their way around the world and making homes of every dwelling.

May we find the strength to plant new roots or take back what we have learnt to where we are from.

Creating new tribes or strengthening old ones.

May we be filled with courage to continue and belief to manifest our visions.

The brave ones.

The warriors.

Brave enough to walk away from a world they don't want and forge something new.

The Brave old souls for the Brave new world......

✦

We are not dicks at heart.
We are beautiful light loving beings,
covered in a mask of defence mechanisms,
triggered wounds and energetic patterns and blocks.
Let nature and truth bring you back home,
again and again..........

✦

Accept each other, Love changes everything.

✦

Everything is ok

The nature told me so
This fear your feeling in your chest
Is excitement don't you know
This is just the beginning
There is so much more in store
Lightworkers been in training years,
There's no time like this before...
Don't worry don't be restless
The good times are ahead
Just breathe and feel and ask for help
Don't suffer alone instead
We each have our part to play
Even the ancestors long gone
Some down in the trenches
Some from the sidelines cheering on
Don't listen to the mayhem
Don't be triggered into fear
And if you do just breathe and feel
And express all there is to clear
Your body is your temple
Your vibe a shining light
Your laughter is pure medicine
And holding loved ones tight
We will look back on this process
We will remember all these years
Will you say you did your part

To let go of all those fears….?
We are each accountable
We are each sovereign and free
This is your soul's journey
For freedom for you and me

✦

When you step behind the veil... deep behind your subconscious, to see the tinted lensed glasses you never knew you were wearing this whole time. An imprint of experience from the past that energetically bent your whole perception. Breathing up behind it, so close you can touch it, not yet making distance.... breathing up around it. Feeling into its presence. It's sensations. It's tensions stored throughout the body. You step back..... and continue to breathe shake it off and relax.

Opening up to a new reality........

✦

Life..... squeezing me, shaping me,

At times feels like I'm being squeezed through tight caves of emotion,

Staying oh so present...feeling and showing compassion, for all these inner feelings inside of me.

Now and again I surface able to rest a while and appreciate, basking in the beauty of the latest Rebirth.

Before diving back down.....

But each time I surface — I am walking more free,

Free from the internalised criticism and voices of the past, echoing thru my inner chambers...

More space to breathe, more energy to move...

Manipulating my energy more and more to move all in the same direction.

Supporting my every step...

Getting behind myself at last...

This is love. This is connection. I am life.

✦

Let us rise in the evolution of who we are.

Women...

How are you treating your inner masculine?

Turn to him

Do you know where he is ?!! Where is he ?!!

Is he forgotten ?

Hiding under a rock or a floorboard ?

Having been projected upon — from our angry sides we still can't contain ??

Or from our withdrawn ways when we get everything we want, but still something creeps in like a niggle ?

Needing someone to blame for our dissatisfaction

Has he been placated ?

Or ignored ?

Shamed

Silenced ??

Some forgotten fragmented part

Left to carry around our bags or pick up the bills or massage us when we're aching

Where is he ?!!! Find him my god

Give him water

Give him rest... attention... fuck what does he need ?!

Who even knew he was in there ?!!?!??! My god !!!

Ok so now let's take him in

Give him a seat at the damn table

Ask him how he is

Be patient

Whatever state he's in

Give him a safe space to recover
All the time he needs
Let him write paint rock
Just hold space for him
Soon in the night you might hear screams
Love him anyway
Nurture him
With all these expectations
These disappointments
Rescue him from the inside first...
Take back our own inner balance.
Then we can give the masculine on the outside world the
space he needs to get his own shit together.

✦

Processing the shadow, bringing in the light
— what are you spelling? Magic is happening constantly...

✦

I am envisioning a mass awakening and uncovering of all that is truth… I let go of any urges to "help" others and move more into a space of trust… I trust all beings are capable of sovereignty and self government over their own energies… I trust every being will be moving more into a flow state, accepting the lessons they are experiencing… surrendering to the teachings and the challenges that they are presented with… with grace, strength and new found awareness… love and trust. I have every faith that each being will be drawn to the teachers that they need in each moment, and are fully supported in their own awakening. Teachers being found also in nature, in silence and inner guidance… we are each our own teacher, student and master. We all have the power to overcome… I let go again and again of any distorted energies and release any emotions with grace… I call upon my ancestors to guide me and great spirit to guide us all. We are in very sensitive times… each thought… each word (what are we spelling…?) What are we giving power to? We can all walk ourselves home and step into a new world.…I have every faith we can each be REBORN.

✦

We need the lows to reach for the highs…
We need weakness to ask for strength…
We need sickness to truly want health…
We need loneliness to seek companionship…
We need the pain to look for the love…
Life is about the CONTRAST
We need boredom to imagine new adventures…
To stretch the imagination…
To evolve and grow, each time seeking more, reaching
further, expanding and creating…
Accepting the fluidity of it all….
Enjoying the ride….

The expansion of consciousness
From within patriarchal structures
The church bells still ring
Castle walls still stand
And battle ground is imprinted on the land
Bringing light to all the wounding
Love to all that's sore
While birds still sing
And sun still shines
It's exciting what's in store
New awareness is awaking,
New light is pouring in
If you listen very faintly it's the new earth coming in.........

✦

Can we stretch our minds to see all points of view and hold all polarity with love..... expanding our minds and giving love to it all........ trying to see the birds eye view over the fragmented society we live amongst ///
Divide and conquer..... ///
Come together and............LOVE.

✦

World on our shoulders

heavy like boulders
pressure to achieve
to succeed
to build a new planet
or to join in the greed
we're a broken generation
tired nation
here to make change
but were stuck in stagnation
future generations will build, but on us is to heal
the importance of healing
it starts with the feeling
not distracting, reacting
blaming and attacking
......WE NEED TO HEAL.
This isn't some hippy dippy deal
casting our shadows onto our kids
subconsciously repeating patterns
ego strengthening
suffering lengthening
narcissistic behaviour
waiting for some saviour
the saviour is within
baby steps on broken paths
reparenting our way back
start again,

never too late to heal, ...to feel
change starts from within
what will it take for you to begin ??

Could all these crises be just a distraction to our
own personal evolution ?
whilst we are kept in fear //
or in judgment of others
or in blame
or in clapping on Thursdays and painting rainbows...
maybe the real distraction is from our own souls journey at
this important time
whilst the earth vibration shifts, we are awakening faster
could this be the distraction of all distractions ?
If we look at our strong reactions
the real next step for Earths growth is here
turn inward
stay in your own lane
be with whats charging up inside of you
feel it
where have we felt this strong feeling before in our lives ?
go deeper
feel deep and clear deep emotions and stuck energies
create more space for light
vibrate higher
process the past
process emotions
process energies
your energy is your participation in this world
this will happen with or without your awareness,
that I am sure

but you can choose to evolve
beautifully
gracefully
with great strength and precision
with self love and gaining wisdom
turn in turn in
turn on
and tune in......

✦

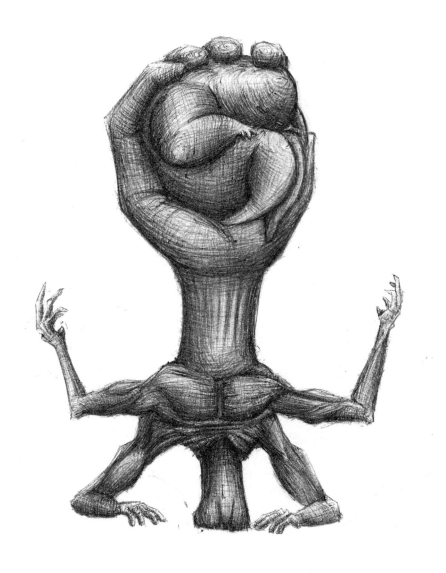

Nothing has changed except everything...

◆

Your comfort zone

Your idle throne
Your gloating smile
No need to moan
Looking down
On all around
Because you've found
This place of known

But what you miss
Is endless bliss
In growth that's found
From all around
From discomfort
From the pain
From the boredom
There's no shame

A magic spark
Hidden in the dark
Things can be grown
From the unknown
Oh no your missing
So much blissing
By remaining in your comfort zone.

✦

It takes a lot of strength to forgive someone
Who never said I'm sorry...

✦

Awareness flooding my whole being

breathing in
breathing out
I am here right now
breathing and feeling
being with whatever is present inside of me
calling all my energy back
looking all around
feeling into my skin container
breathing into it all
breathing in
breathing out
I am here right now
I am here right now
I am here right now

✦

Can you see beyond the behaviour to see the soul
beneath?
Old souls written into difficult stories
dense with pain and suffering
head under water
struggling to survive
some tireless urge to stay alive
an ongoing battle
trying to finally thrive...//

✦

Emotions clouding your judgment

Like huge tidal waves
Taking you under
dragging you down
swirling beneath the surface
Unable to see clearly
Take space — to let the sands settle again.
before making your next move.

✦

When you have cradled fragmented parts of your
soul, and sung them back together…
You will realise a love for your own self
That is so precious and pure,
That no sex drugs and rock n roll could ever endure…
When you see full on your souls strength, courage and
determination
You will gasp in the reflection of your own beauty
You will never give any part of yourself away again so
freely…
You will become very choosing on who to share this sacred
energy with…

This energy that can heal Planets…

✦

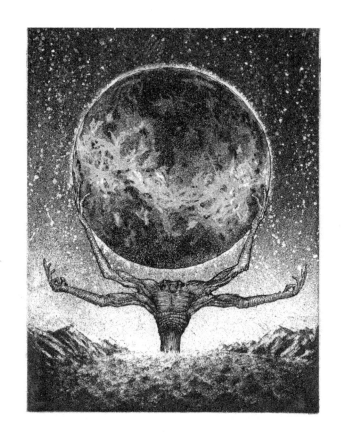

ABOUT THE AUTHOR

After realising early on how she was not compatible to the current system, Lisa embarked upon a 10 year journey around the world trying to put herself back together from a build up of trauma in her body & mind. She began studying intensely different healing methods, ancient yogic practices & her own inner world. She has become over the years fascinated with the way we can release the body from tightly held traumas through many methods, her favourites being Breathwork, Massage, Yoga and Dance.

And also through the power of telling our stories to make sense of the past. She has always known writing to be a powerful healer, with diaries stretching back to her younger years, all stacked away underneath her bed...First inspired in English class... A secret hidden artist.

From her depression Photography sprouted allowing her to express herself through the beauty she saw on her travels. A young love helped her to start seeing life in colour, then healing awakened her voice. Poetry became a way where she channeled her emotions into

self expression and often rhymed word. Touching the hearts of many she comprised it all into this book. Too dark and beautiful to be lost in past posts of Instagram.
Forever now in print.
She has created her healing workshop the Breath Ceremony which she has been travelling the world with for the years preceding lockdown in some massive festivals healing areas. But now she is residing in middle England, working hard from her cocoon to inspire a new world.

Watch out for her next 2 books due to be released very soon "Breathing back to life" and "Gypsy souls : a Twin Flame journey"

Printed in Great Britain
by Amazon

22284900R00118